Welcome to Inky Garden!

Open the pages to a fantastical range of illustrations to suit your mood; from scenes with depth, to mandalas and cute garden visitors… to more artistic illustrations. Plus! Quests, and items to make including a 3D paper flower to colour and fold!

Throughout these pages are five, four-leaf clovers. Find them on your colouring journey, and I hope they bring you luck.

Every hand-drawn detail was created with care and love. I aimed to achieve adequately sized spaces within the designs to offer you an enjoyable experience (not so small that it's too difficult to colour) and also include areas where you can loosen up your wrist a little; to colour, shade, or embellish.

Large illustrations are single-sided (smaller embellishments on the left side) in case you wish to use pens when colouring, or tear out to use or display. I would suggest placing a blank sheet under the page if you are using certain pens - to protect the illustration beneath.

Some illustrations are portrait and some landscape way round to suit the book format.

I hope you enjoy the book as much as I did making it for you!

Happy colouring!

Find 5 of these clovers in your book...

This book belongs to

Write your favourite herb on the cork

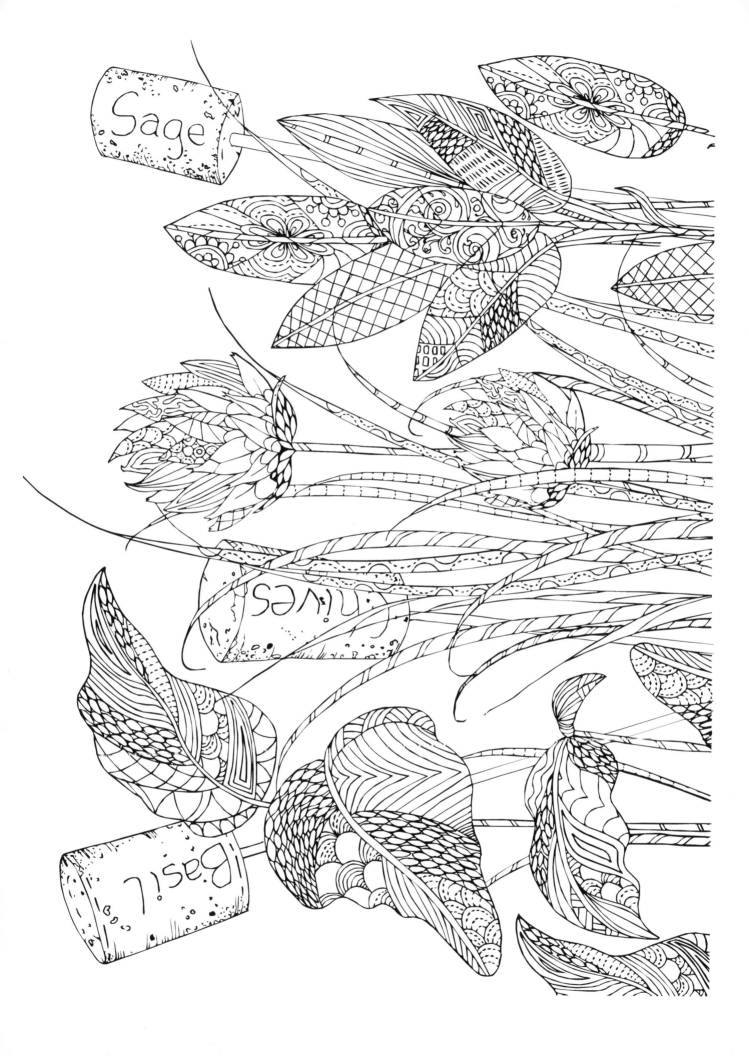

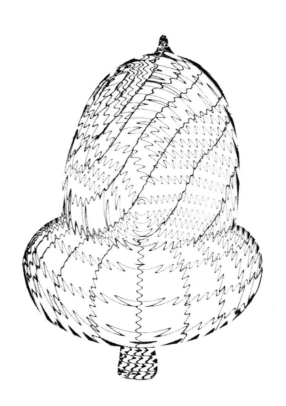

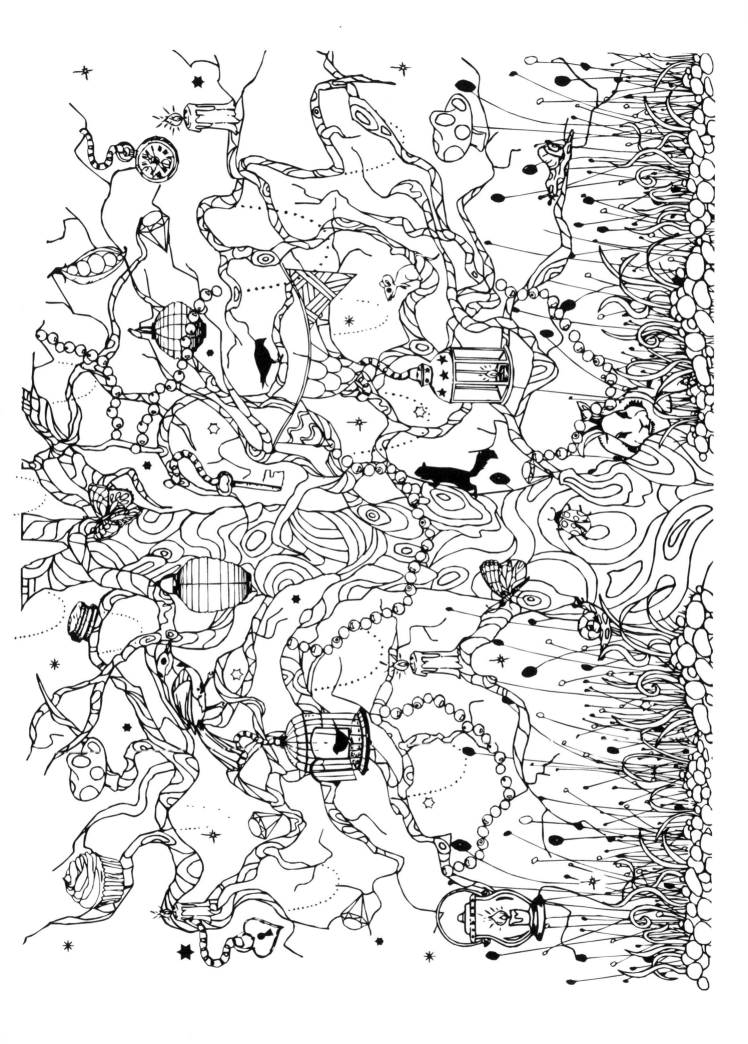

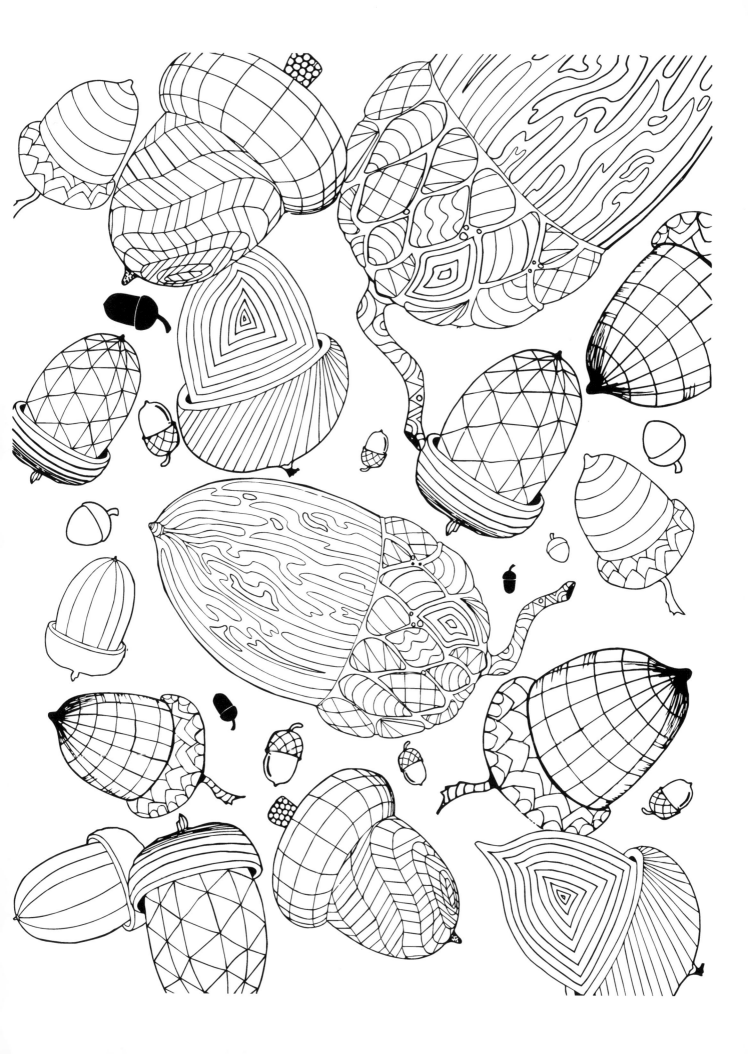

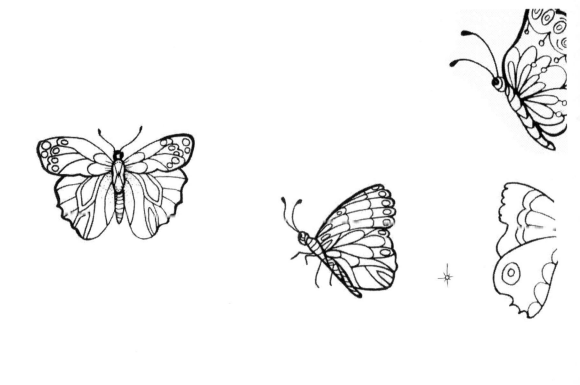

Write your name on the garden sign opposite…

Add lots of colour to the flowerbed…

Barn Swallow eggs...

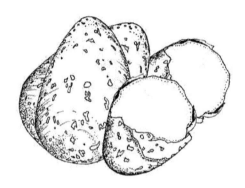

Add delicate colour

A well-earned tea and cake break…

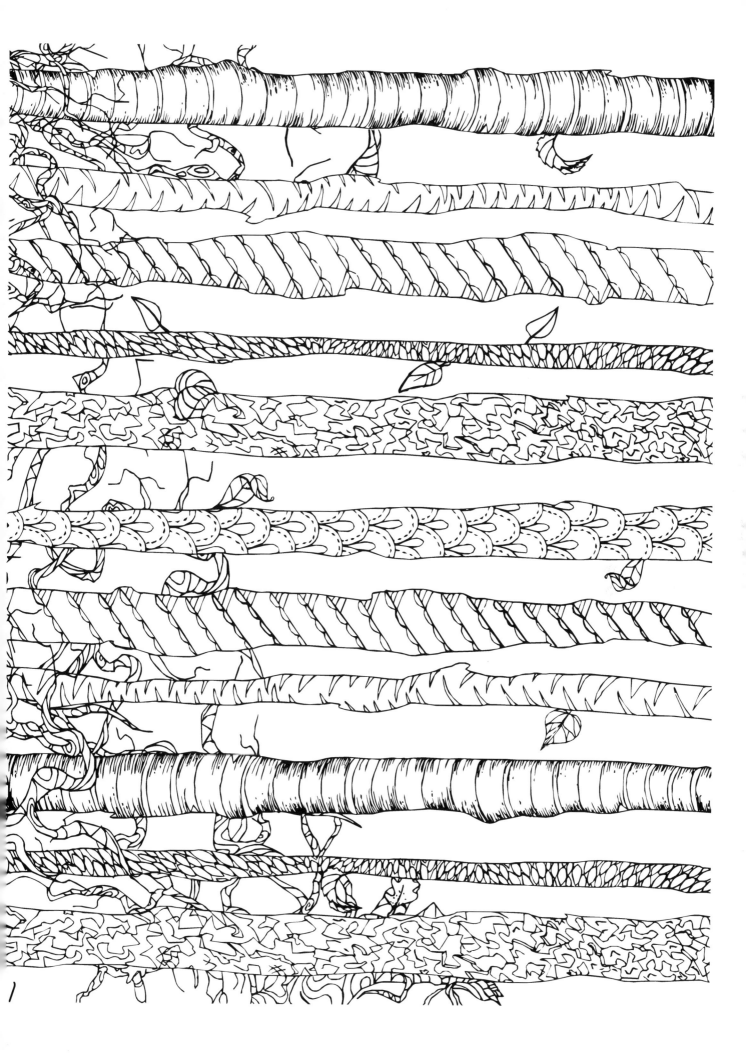

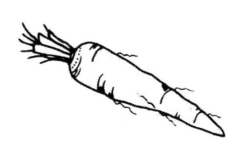

Help the bee create a trail of honey drops to the hive.

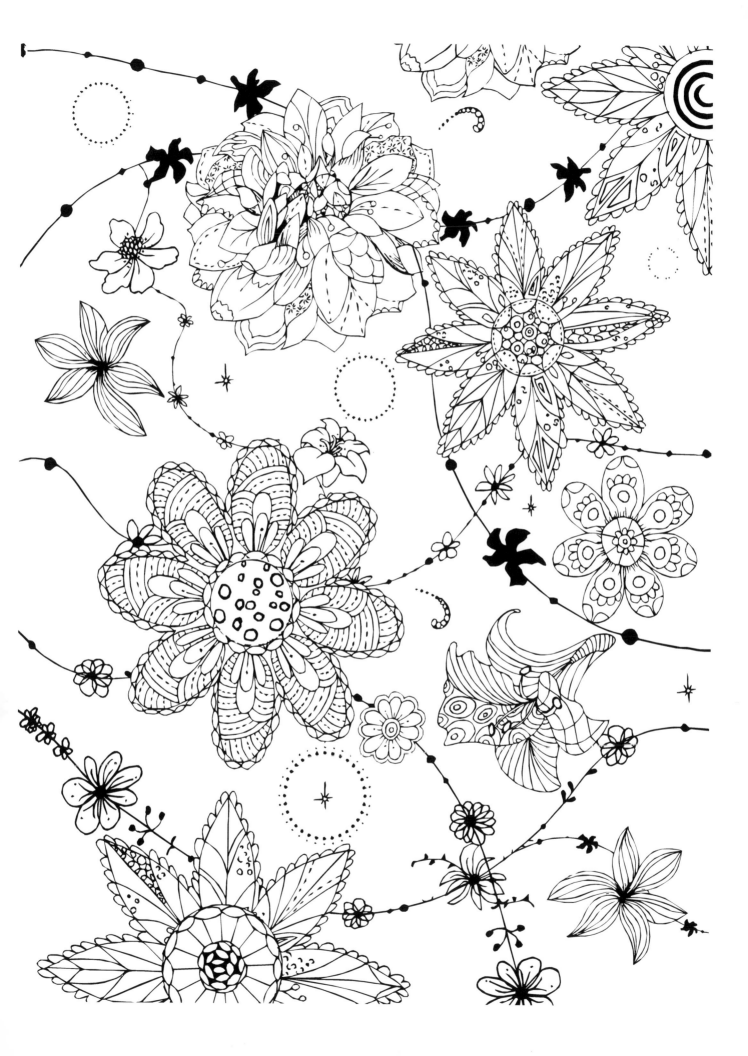

Add pretty petals to the flower centres
to complete the garden scene opposite.

Make a wish

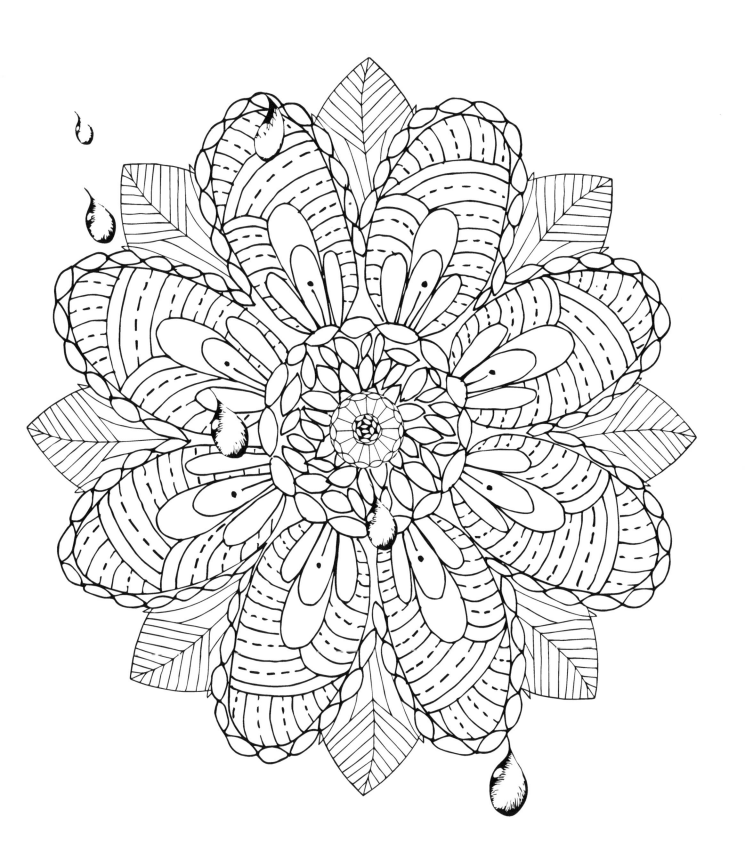

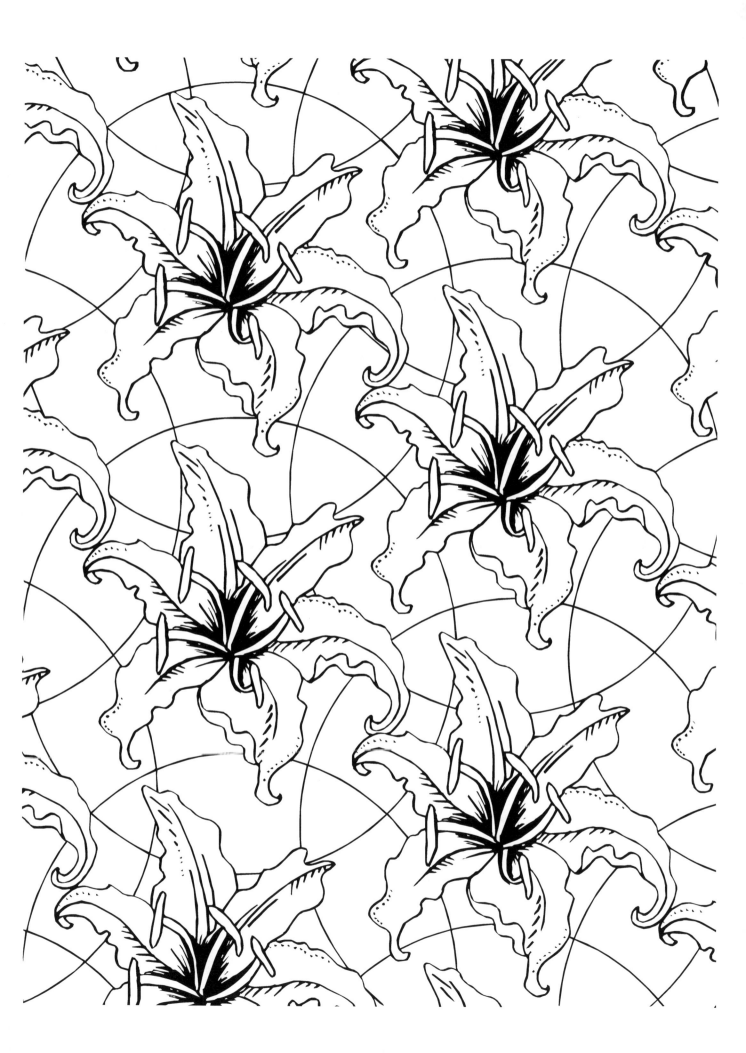

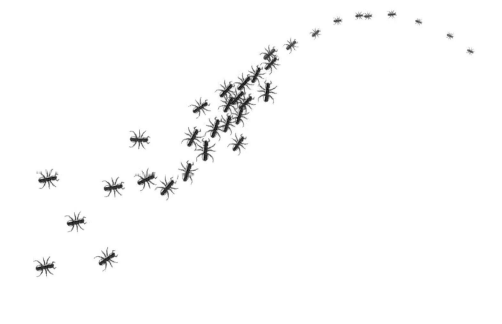

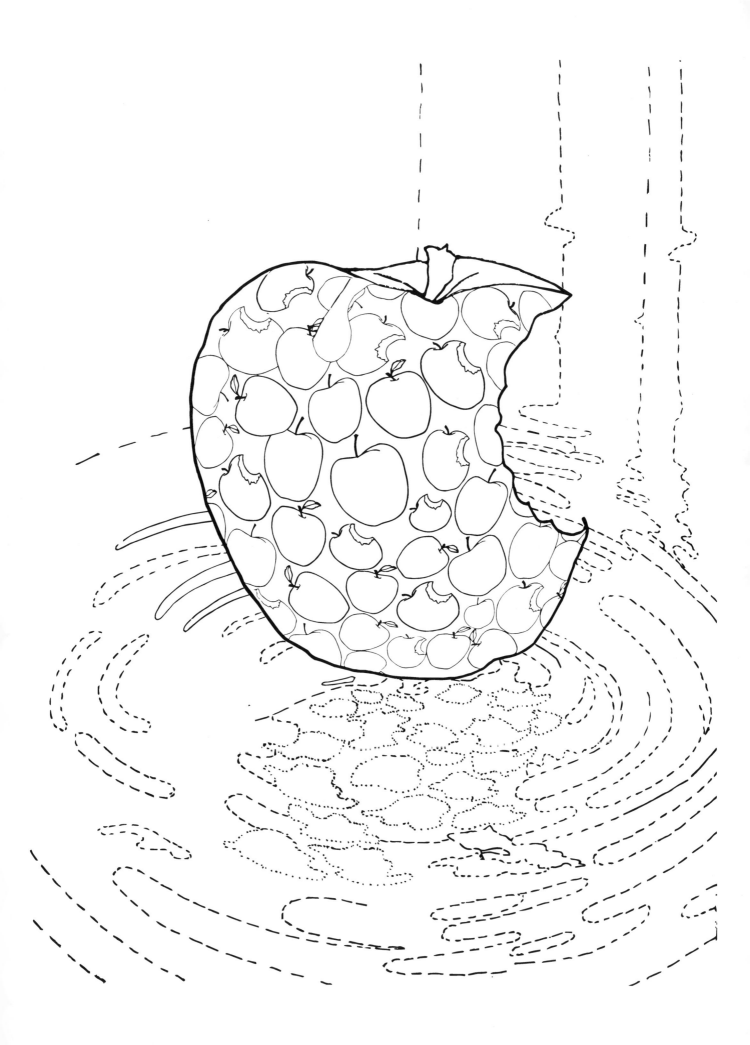

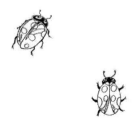

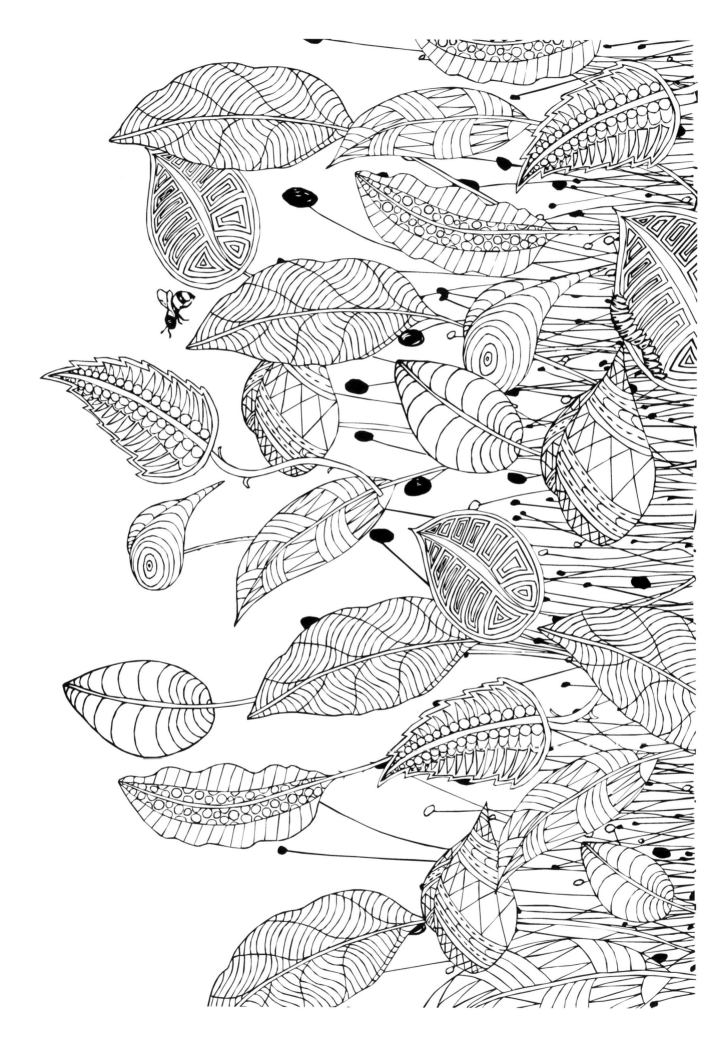

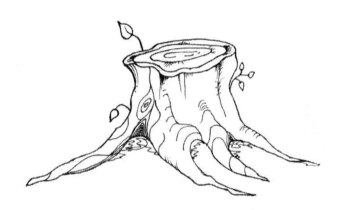

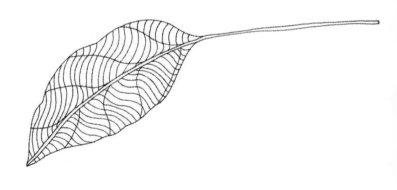

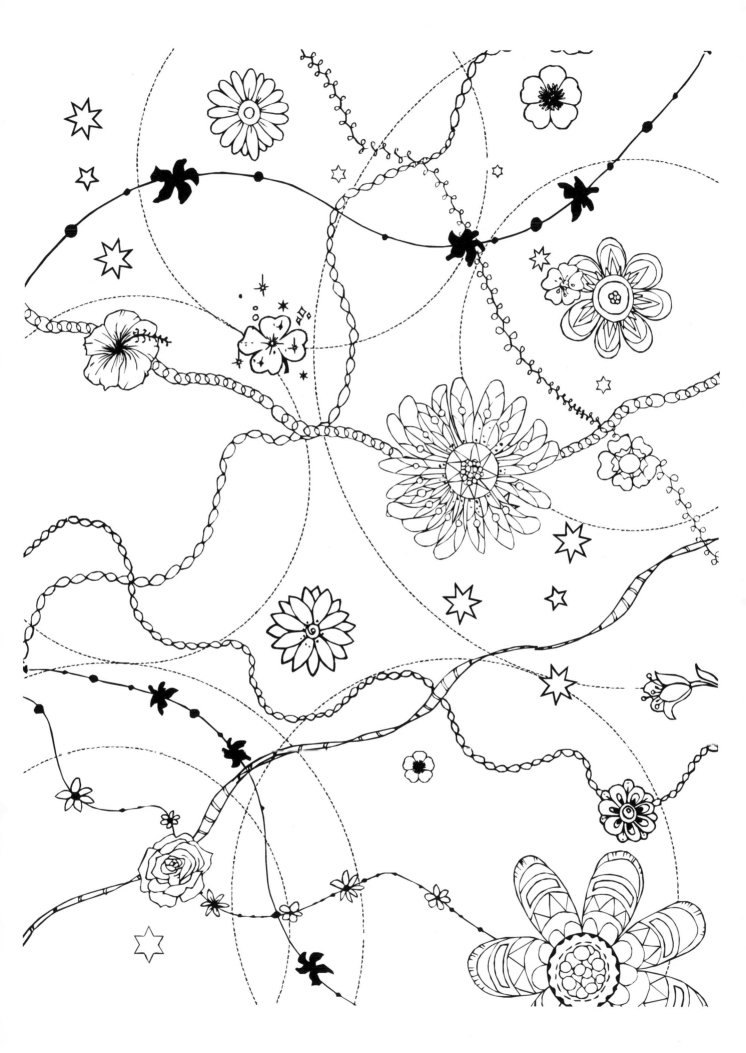

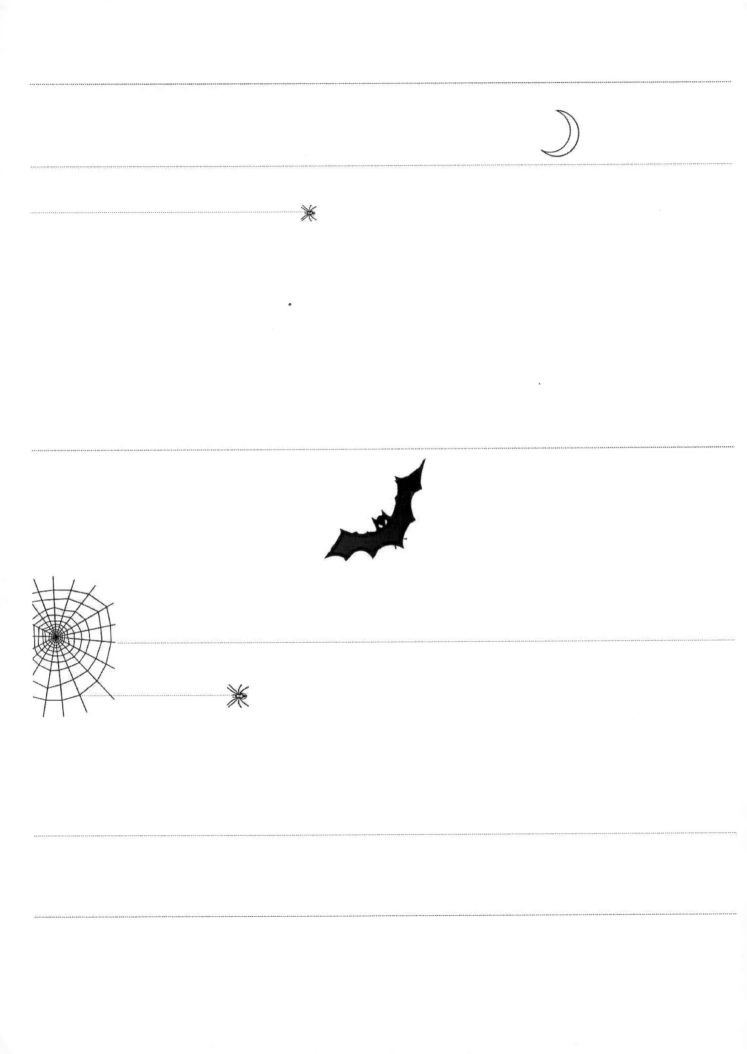

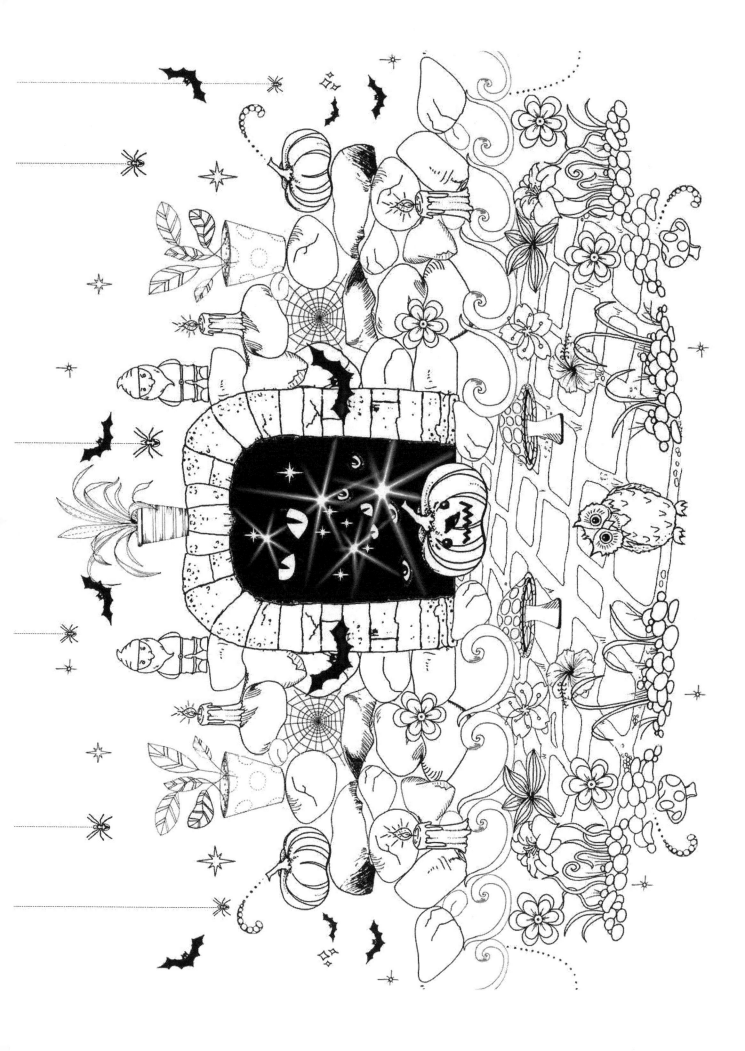

Fill in the missing items to complete the sequences opposite…
(Answers at the end of the book)

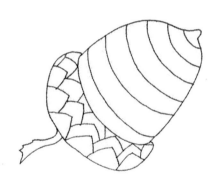

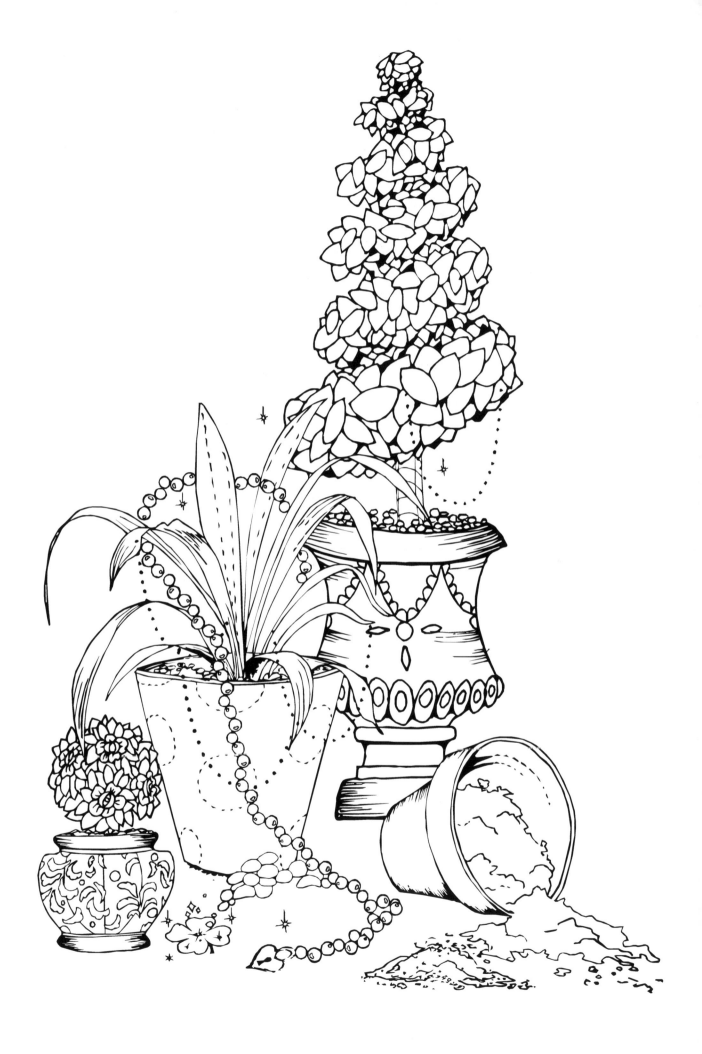

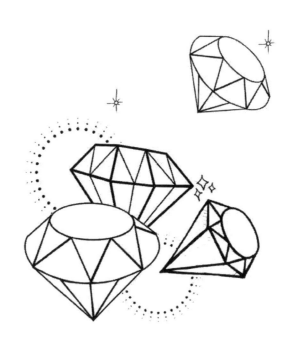

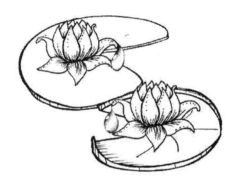

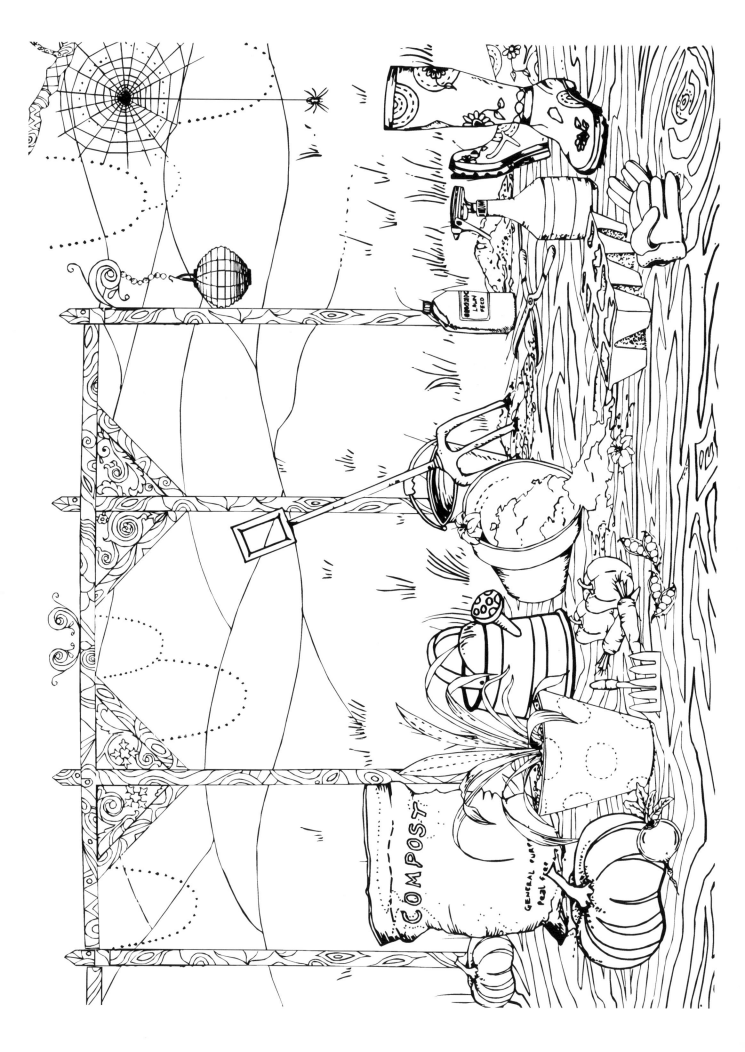

Colour and fold your own 3D paper flower!

Colour the patterned areas of the five petals and butterfly
on the next six pages.
Then follow the instructions at the end of the book
to bring your flower to life!

Colour the butterfly…
ready to cut out, and glue to your 3D flower.

Love to colour...

BOOKMARK

Colour, cut out, then glue a piece of card between the two designs
...or you could laminate and even add a pretty ribbon, beads or charm!

How to fold and glue your 3D flower!   Practice on a blank sheet first.

Cut the petal pages into large squares.   Fold the square up to make a triangle
(Pattern area to be positioned as pic 1... narrow pattern facing you)
Fold up the left flap to meet the top corner point, and crease.
Fold the flap back down in half, so that the edge is
in line with the edge beneath it. (picture 3)

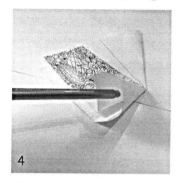  

Open up the flap, (indicated in picture 4)
then spread it open, in half, then flatten.
Fold down the little top flap so that it doesnt stick out. (picture 6)

Fold the whole flap in half, folding inwards.
REPEAT all the steps for the right hand side of the petal.
Bring the two edges together, glue where the inner flaps meet
and secure with a clip while drying. The petal should be curved – don't crease!
Do this for all five petals.
Then glue the petals together and secure with clips while the glue dries.
Glue your butterfly to the centre.   Or to be more creative... attach
the butterfly to a petal and place a gem or button in the centre of the flower!

Did you locate the four-leaf clovers?
These are the pages they are located.

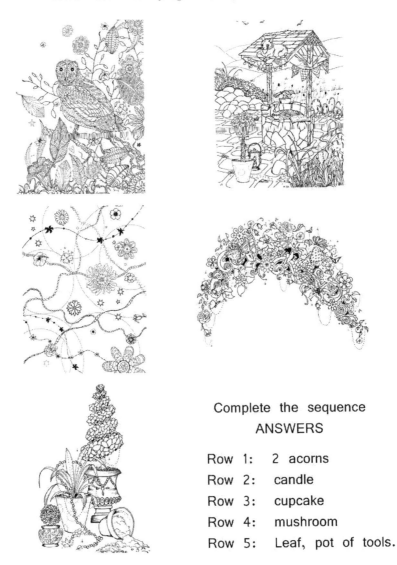

Complete the sequence
ANSWERS

Row 1: 2 acorns
Row 2: candle
Row 3: cupcake
Row 4: mushroom
Row 5: Leaf, pot of tools.

I hope you enjoyed being creative.
Helen. x
For colouring tips, design examples and to discover more, please visit…
www.Helenclaireart.co.uk

Have you tried the other themed books in the Inky series?

Made in the USA
Lexington, KY
08 June 2016